KIDS ON EARTH

Wildlife Adventures – Explore The World
Sea Lion - Ecuador

Sensei Paul David

COPYRIGHT PAGE

Kids On Earth: Wildlife Adventures - Explore The World

Sea Lion - Ecuador

by Sensei Paul David,

Copyright © 2023.

All rights reserved.

978-1-77848-185-7 KoE_WildLife_Amazon_PaperbackBook_ecuador_sea lion

978-1-77848-184-0 KoE_WildLife_Amazon_eBook_ecuador_sea lion

978-1-77848-422-3 KoE_Wildlife_Ingram_Paperbackbook_SeaLion

This book is not authorized for free distribution copying.

www.senseipublishing.com

@senseipublishing
#senseipublishing

Synopsis

This book explores 30 fun facts about the sea lion in Ecuador. It covers topics such as the sea lion's diet, its lifespan, how it communicates, and its role in the marine ecosystem. It also discusses the threats sea lions in Ecuador face from human activities such as fishing, pollution, and climate change. Finally, the book encourages readers to help protect sea lions and keep the ocean healthy.

Get Our FREE Books Now!

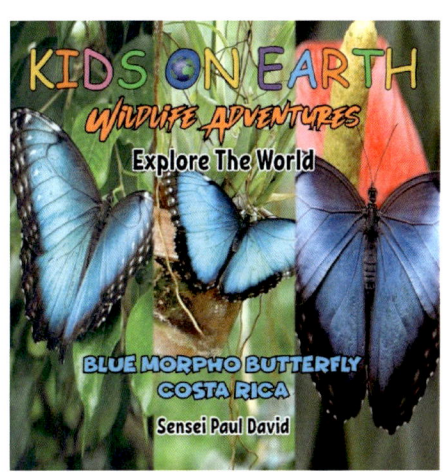

kidsonearth.life

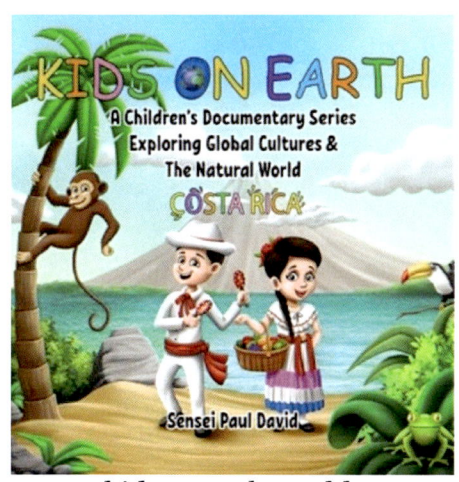

kidsonearth.world

Click Below for Another Book In Each Series

senseipublishing.com/KoE_SERIES

senseipublishing.com/KoE_Wildlife_SERIES

KoE En Español

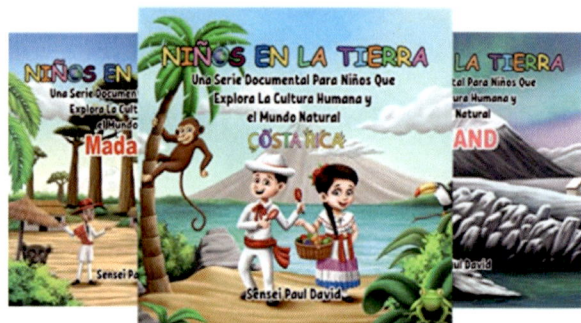

senseipublishing.com/KoE_SERIES_SPANISH

www.senseipublishing.com

Join Our Publishing Journey!

If you would like to receive FUTURE FREE BOOKS and get to know us better, please click www.senseipublishing.com and join our newsletter by entering your email address in the pop-up box.

Follow Our Blog: senseipauldavid.ca

Follow/Like/Subscribe: Facebook, Instagram, YouTube: @senseipublishing

Scan the QR Code with your phone or tablet to follow us on social media:

Like / Subscribe / Follow

Introduction

Welcome to the world of sea lions! Sea lions are fascinating creatures that live in oceans, seas, and rivers all over the world. But today, we're going to focus on sea lions that live in Ecuador. This book will teach you 30 fun facts about the sea lion in Ecuador. So, jump on in and get ready to learn all about the amazing sea lion!

Sea lions in Ecuador typically live for about 20 years.

The Galapagos sea lion is the only species of sea lion found in Ecuador.

Galapagos sea lions are found mainly around the Galapagos Islands.

Sea lions are very social and live in large groups called "hauls".

Sea lions in Ecuador are omnivores, meaning they eat both plants and animals.

Galapagos sea lions can reach up to 8 feet long and weigh up to 600 pounds.

Sea lions in Ecuador come ashore to rest, give birth, and mate.

Sea lions use their whiskers to help them find food in the dark.

Sea lions have a thick layer of blubber which helps them stay warm in the cold ocean water.

Sea lions in Ecuador use vocalizations to communicate with each other.

Sea lions can stay underwater for up to 30 minutes.

Sea lions are excellent swimmers and can swim up to 25 miles per hour.

Sea lions in Ecuador feed mainly on fish, squid, octopus, and crustaceans.

Galapagos sea lions are the smallest species of sea lion.

Sea lions have a thick layer of fur which helps keep them warm and water resistant.

Sea lions in Ecuador are very playful and can be seen playing with each other and with other animals.

Sea lions are able to rotate their hind flippers forward to help them move on land.

Galapagos sea lions are a protected species in Ecuador and are listed as vulnerable by the IUCN.

Sea lions in Ecuador form strong bonds with their mates and often mate for life.

Sea lions are very vocal and can make a variety of sounds including barks, honks, and whistles.

Sea lions in Ecuador are an important part of the marine ecosystem and help to keep the population of fish and other marine animals in balance.

Sea lions have an excellent sense of smell and can detect food from miles away.

Sea lions in Ecuador feed mainly at night when the water is calmer.

Sea lions can dive up to 1,250 feet deep in search of food.

Sea lions give birth to a single pup which is nursed for up to one year.

Sea lions form strong bonds with their pups and will protect them fiercely.

Sea lions in Ecuador are highly intelligent and can be trained to perform tricks.

Sea lions have long whiskers which they use to detect vibrations in the water.

Sea lions in Ecuador are threatened by human activities such as fishing, pollution, and climate change.

Sea lions are an important part of the marine ecosystem and play a vital role in the health of the ocean.

Conclusion

We hope you've learned a lot about the amazing sea lion in Ecuador! These fascinating creatures are a valuable part of the marine ecosystem and play an important role in keeping the ocean healthy. We hope you've enjoyed learning about them and will help to protect them from the threats they face.

Thank you for reading this book!

If you found this book helpful, I would be grateful if you would **post an honest review on Amazon** so this book can reach other supportive readers like you!

All you need to do is digitally flip to the back and leave your review. Or visit amazon.com/author/senseipauldavid click the correct book cover and click on the blue link next to the yellow stars that say, "customer reviews."

As always...

It's a great day to be alive!

Share Our FREE eBooks Now!

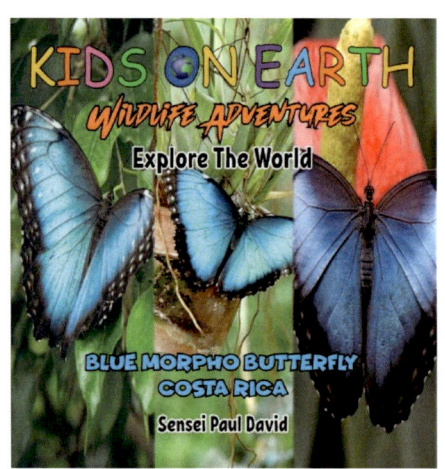

kidsonearth.life

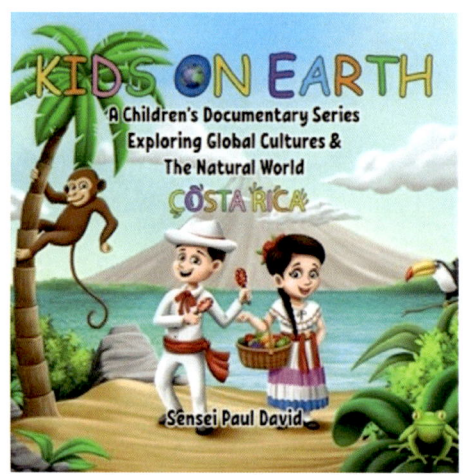

kidsonearth.world

Click Below for Another Book In Each Series

senseipublishing.com/KoE_SERIES

senseipublishing.com/KoE_Wildlife_SERIES

KoE En Español

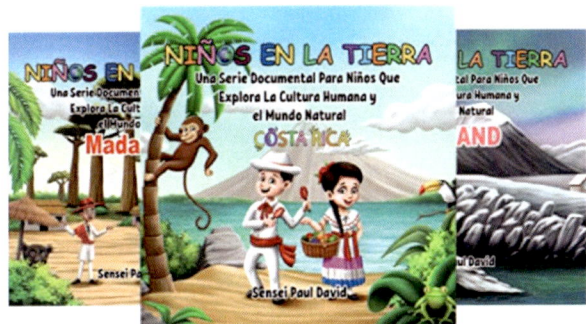

senseipublishing.com/KoE_SERIES_SPANISH

www.senseipublishing.com

www.senseipublishing.com

@senseipublishing
#senseipublishing

Check out our **recommendations** for other books for adults & kids plus other great resources by visiting
www.senseipublishing.com/resources/

Join Our Publishing Journey!

If you would like to receive FREE BOOKS and special offers, please visit www.senseipublishing.com and join our newsletter by entering your email address in the pop-up box

Follow Our Engaging Blog NOW!
senseipauldavid.ca

Get Our FREE Books Today!

Click & Share the Links Below

FREE Kids Books

lifeofbailey.senseipublishing.com
kidsonearth.senseipublishing.com

FREE Self-Development Book

senseiselfdevelopment.senseipublishing.com

FREE BONUS!!!
Experience Over 25 FREE Engaging Guided Meditations!

Prized Skills & Practices for Adults & Kids. Help Restore Deep Sleep, Lower Stress, Improve Posture, Navigate Uncertainty & More.

Download the Free Insight Timer App and click the link below:
http://insig.ht/sensei_paul

About Sensei Publishing

Sensei Publishing commits itself to helping people of all ages transform into better versions of themselves by providing high-quality and research-based self-development books with an emphasis on mental health and guided meditations. Sensei Publishing offers well-written e-books, audiobooks, paperbacks, and online courses that simplify complicated but practical topics in line with its mission to inspire people toward positive transformation.

It's a great day to be alive!

About the Author

I create simple & transformative eBooks & Guided Meditations for Adults & Children proven to help navigate uncertainty, solve niche problems & bring families closer together.

I'm a former finance project manager, private pilot, jiu-jitsu instructor, musician & former University of Toronto Fitness Trainer. I prefer a science-based approach to focus on these & other areas in my life to stay humble & hungry to evolve. I hope you enjoy my work and I'd love to hear your feedback.

- It's a great day to be alive!
Sensei Paul David

Scan & Follow/Like/Subscribe: Facebook, Instagram, YouTube: @senseipublishing

Scan using your phone/iPad camera for Social Media
Visit us at www.senseipublishing.com and sign up for our newsletter to learn more about our exciting books and to experience our FREE Guided Meditations for Kids & Adults.

www.ingramcontent.com/pod-product-compliance
Lightning Source LLC
Chambersburg PA
CBRC090902080526
44587CB00008B/170